These Islands:
New Zealand

These Islands

Photographs, text and design by Mike Calder, unless otherwise stated.

Published by
    Mike Calder Photography
        mjcalder@bigpond.com
        www.mikecalder.co.nz

Distributed by
    Allphy Book Distributors Limited
        4 Charles Street, Eden Terrace, Auckland
        ph 0-9-623 4301
        fax 0-9-623 4485
        books@allphy.co.nz

Calder, Mike.
        These Islands: New Zealand
        ISBN 978-0-473-12377-2

Thank you Jane, Jenny and David for your love and support

Previous Page: Sunset on Omata Beach, New Plymouth

Printed in China by Everbest

These Islands: New Zealand

About 25 million years ago, tectonic movements began to pull New Zealand apart from the great Southern continent Gondwana. Striding the precarious boundary of the Pacific and Indo-Australian plates, New Zealand's dramatic, dynamic landscape is still being shaped. On the North Island, several volcanoes are active and the Southern Alps, which form the backbone of the South Island are still being lifted skywards.

Adrift on this raft in the South Pacific, a unique ecosystem developed. There were no land-dwelling mammals, so this niche was filled by flightless birds such as the Moa (now extinct) and the kiwi. Of the plants in New Zealand, 80% occur only in New Zealand.

The first settlers arrived from Eastern Polynesia some time between AD 800 and 1300, making it one of the most recently-settled lands on Earth. They named it "Aotearoa", meaning "the land of the long white cloud". Over time these people developed their own distinct Maori culture.

The arrival of Europeans in the 18th century brought the inevitable clash of cultures. Although the Treaty of Waitangi in 1840 between Britain and Maori chiefs provided for the protection of Maoris and their resources, alienation of Maori land occurred well into the 20th century and led to the decline of Maori culture. Fortunately this has undergone a recent revival and is now seen as fundamental to New Zealand's culture as a whole.

Today most of the 4.2 million people who call New Zealand home live in modern cities in a prosperous, multi-cultural society. 68% are of European origin, 15% Maori, 10% Asian and 7% Pacific Islanders. They are a resourceful, enterprising, adventurous, socially progressive and independent people, justifiably proud of their achievements.

In this book I have attempted to convey some of the unique features of *These Islands: New Zealand*. I hope you enjoy reading it.

Mike

Auckland

Sandwiched on a narrow isthmus of land between the Pacific Ocean and the Tasman Sea, Auckland is tucked between two harbours and virtually surrounded by sea. Not surprisingly, it has the highest per capita ownership of boats and yachts in the world and is dubbed the 'City of Sails'.

The city sits on top of a dormant volcanic field and the 50 volcanic vents in the area take the form of landmarks such as cones, lagoons, lakes and islands.

Maoris settled in the Auckland area as early as 1350, their population peaking at around 20,000 before the arrival of Europeans in the 1830s. It became the capital of New Zealand in 1840, but lost this title to Wellington in 1865.

Today one third of New Zealand's 4 million people live in Auckland. It is a bustling, vibrant, cosmopolitan city with the largest Polynesian population in the world. 11% of its residents are Maori, 14% are of Pacific Island descent, 19% are Asian and the remaining 56% are of European origin.

Auckland

Towering 328 metres above the city, Auckland's Sky Tower is the tallest in the Southern Hemisphere. The views from the four viewing platforms are superb.

Auckland's CBD adjoins Waitemata Harbour, a deep-water port and home of the 1999-2000 and 2002-2003 America's Cup challenges. From here a short ferry trip across to historical Devonport rewards you with glorious views back to the city.

Two surfers check out the conditions at Piha (right), one of Auckland's most popular surf beaches and typical of the rugged, black-sand beaches of the west coast.

Northland

Northland is rich in history and some of the earliest traces of Maori settlement can be found here. It was where contact between Maori and European settlers first occured and where New Zealand's most important document, the Treaty of Waitangi was signed between the British Crown and a number of Maori chiefs. New Zealand's most northerly point, Cape Reinga is regarded by Maori as being the departing point for spirits of the dead. Northland's natural beauty includes green rolling farmland, dense Kauri forests, white sandy beaches and picturesque bays like Urquharts Bay, pictured here.

The Coromandel Peninsula

The Coromandel Peninsula juts north into the Pacific Ocean, 85 kilometres long and 40 kilometres at its widest point, protecting the Hauraki Gulf and Auckland from the elements. The rugged, rainforest-cloaked Coromandel Range forms a dramatic spine for the peninisula, rising to 900 metres in height. Surrounding the range are lush farmlands and protected harbours, such as Tairua Harbour (top). The beautiful white sandy beaches on the east coast make the peninsula a favourite holiday destination for New Zealanders. Coromandel Town (bottom) is one of only five small towns on the peninsula.

The Waikato Region

Hamilton is New Zealand's fourth largest urban area and largest inland city, straddling the mighty Waikato River (right), at 425km the longest in the country. The city is a rapidly-growing farming, financial and educational centre. The extensive Hamilton Gardens features authentic theme gardens such as the Japanese Garden of Contemplation (bottom centre) and the Italian Renaissance Garden (bottom right).

Waitomo has two landscapes: rich, green rolling farmland above ground and an intricate network of caves formed when water percolating down through cracks in the limestone formed an underground drainage system. At the Mangapohue Natural Bridge, a spectacular double arch has been formed by the collapse of a cave roof.

The Waikato Region

New Zealand has many fine surfing beaches, none better than those at Raglan which are world-renowned for their left hand breaks, some of the best and longest in the world. Ruapuke Beach (left) has hosted a world championship surfing event and is typical of the beautiful black-sand beaches on the west coast. The colour of the sand is due to the abundance of iron-rich minerals in the sand.

Taranaki

The near-perfect symmetrical volcanic cone of Mt Taranaki/Egmont dominates the surrounding rich dairy cattle country of the Taranaki Region. At 2518m, the dormant Mt Taranaki/Egmont is the second-tallest mountain on the North Island and last erupted in 1755.

New Plymouth, the commercial centre of the region received a boost with the discovery of natural gas in the 1970s. The city boasts one of New Zealand's finest parks, an innovative museum and many beautiful beaches. On the waterfront the 45m Wind Wand sculpture sways in the breeze.

Hawke's Bay

The Hawke's Bay region is regarded as the fruit bowl of New Zealand, with extensive orchards and vineyards catering for the burgeoning wine industry. On February 3rd 1931 the district was devastated by an earthquake, killing 258 people and reducing Napier and Hastings to rubble. Napier grasped the opportunity, widening its streets and designing its buildings in the Art Deco style (below).

At Cape Kidnappers there are 5,000 pairs of gannets, making it the world's largest mainland gannet colony. At around 15 weeks, young gannets fly 3,000km to Australia, where they spend a couple of years before returning for the rest of their lives to New Zealand.

Lake Taupo and Tongariro National Park

A massive volcanic eruption in AD 186 spewed out about 30 cubic km of rock and ash and formed Lake Taupo, New Zealand's largest lake, 616 sq km in area and 186m deep. The lake is drained by the Waikato River, which narrows from 100m across to 15m before plunging over the Huka Falls (below) in a display of awesome power. At the southern end of the lake lies Tongariro National Park with its three active volcanoes: Ruapehu, Ngauruhoe and Tongariro. The Emerald Lakes (far right) are passed on the Tongariro Crossing, described by many as the best one-day walk in New Zealand.

Rotorua

The early Maori settlers in Rotorua were no doubt attracted to the area by the thermal activity. They used the hot pools for cooking (top right) and bathing, while the warm earth kept them warm during the winters. In the late 19th century the geothermal attractions began to draw an increasing number of tourists and in 1908 the largest bath house in the Southern Hemisphere opened. That impressive building now houses the Rotorua Museum of Art and History (top left). Today Rotorua is the North Island's most popular tourist attraction, visitors are attracted to the geysers, boiling mud pools, heated mineral pools and lakes of the district.

Maori culture has survived well in Rotorua, offering visitors an insight into Maori history, art, architecture and way of life.

Geothermal Areas

For about 20 million years New Zealand has been straddling two of the world's fifteen tectonic plates. In the North Island, the Pacific Plate passes under the Australian Plate, creating the Taupo Volcanic Zone, one of the most active geothermal areas in the world. It is about 50 km wide and 300 km long, and contains volcanoes, hot springs and geysers. Deposition of minerals dissolved in the waters around hot springs create varied and beautiful colours, such as around the gorgeous Champagne Pool at Wai-O-Tapu (far right) and the Warbrick Terrace at Waimangu (below). Geysers like the Lady Knox Geyser (right) are formed when surface water seeps down through the ground, becomes superheated and is ejected through the spout. In the South Island, the Australian Plate pushes under the Pacific Plate, pushing up the Southern Alps.

Wellington

Wellington replaced Auckland as the capital city of New Zealand in 1865. The nation's second-largest city has 400,000 residents and is not only the political and administrative centre of government, but proudly promotes itself as the arts and cultural capital; being home to the national museum, Te Papa Tongarewa; the film and theatre industry and numerous other galleries and national organisations.

Sandwiched between the surrounding mountains and picturesque Wellington Harbour, with its ever-changing mood, it is a compact city. Major earthquakes in 1848 and 1855 lifted some of the harbour out of the sea, and much of the CBD has been built on that reclaimed land. The area still experiences regular seismic activity.

Wellington

Because of the earthquake risk, early buildings in Wellington were constructed of wood. The beautiful Old St Paul's Church (bottom left) was constructed from native timbers in 1845 and served as the Anglican Cathedral for 98 years.

The distinctively-designed Beehive building and next door Parliament building (bottom right) house the executive and parliamentary wings of government.

Construction of the cable car (top right) began in 1901. Three tunnels were blasted and dug by hand and by 1912 it was carrying a million passengers a year. Electricity replaced steam in 1933 and today it is still carrying commuters and tourists from the CBD to the university and botanical gardens (top left).

The Maori

New Zealand is one of the last habitable parts of Earth to be settled. Several waves of people from Eastern Polynesia arrived between AD 800 and 1300 and over time developed a culture derived from their roots. They found a land with abundant bird and marine life, but after several centuries resources became stretched and warfare became more common. Early explorers like Abel Tasman and James Cook described the Maori as a proud and fierce warrior race.

In 1840 the Treaty of Waitangi was signed between the British Crown and 500 Maori chiefs, making the Maori British subjects in return for a guarantee of property rights and autonomy. However by 1890 the Maori had lost 90% of their land and were in decline as a race. By the 1960s most were urbanised and they were losing their cultural identity. Fortunately, since then Maori culture has undergone a revival and is integral to the identity of New Zealand.

The Maori religion conceives that all natural elements and living things are connected and possess a life force or mauri. They share myths of the creation of the universe, gods and people with other Polynesian people.

A marae (meeting house) is the centre of a community. Here Maori language is spoken and ceremonies such as weddings and funerals take place. Older people impart Maori traditions and cultural practices including legends, songs and traditional arts such as carving and weaving.

Art is an important part of Maori culture, often expressed in the form of carvings on houses, canoes and weapons. A moko is a body carving, men traditionally receive moko on their faces, buttocks and thighs, while women wear one on their lips and chin.

A hangi is the traditional, flavoursome way of cooking food. A hole is dug, the fire lit and stones are heated; when they are hot, the food is placed on top and covered over with leaves or mats. Finally soil covers everything to keep the heat in.

The haka was a war dance, performed before battle to fortify the warriors and hopefully frighten the enemy. This fearsome chant is now performed regularly by national rugby teams before a match.

Bird Life

kiwi

weka

Prior to the arrival of humans, the only mammals in New Zealand were three species of bats and the ground-dwelling niche was taken by flightless birds, such as the kiwi and weka. These shy birds were no match for the introduced mammals and are now endangered.

The kea is a parrot, known as the clown of the mountains due to its antics and familiarity with humans. They were nearly hunted to extinction, but are now protected and there are between 1,000 and 5,000 birds left.

The wandering albatross has the largest wingspan of any bird in the world, at about 3 metres. It can effortlessly wander over 500 km per day and 56,000 km per year at speeds ranging from 50 - 90 km per hour.

Plant Life

beech forest

totara

kauri

silver fern

New Zealand was once part of the supercontinent Gondwana, which included most of the land masses in today's southern hemisphere. It shares species in common with these lands, such as totara and beech trees, but after it broke away about 20 million years ago a unique variety of flora evolved. The majority of plants are evergreen, flowers are typically small and white, they are not fire-resistant and very few have any defence against introduced mammals.

Although green on top, the silver fern's leaves are a bright silver underneath. It is on New Zealand's coat of arms and has become the emblem of the country's cricket, rugby and netball teams.

The kauri tree once flourished across the land. It was so prized for its timber that in 1853 it comprised 31% of the nation's exports. In the few remaining stands of this magnificent tree, the largest ones are over 1,000 years old.

Fungi

In Autumn, an amazing variety of fungi can be seen in the forests. What we see is just the fruiting body of a fungus, 90% or more of it exists as a network of microscopically thin threads in the soil. Unlike plants, fungi do not make their food, they need existing organic matter to survive. While some grow only on dead wood, others can only survive on living material.

Marlborough

Many visitors to Marlborough arrive on the ferry from Wellington through a wonderful labyrinth of sheltered bays, secluded inlets, islands and peninsulas that make up the Marlborough Sounds. Much of this collection of three drowned river valleys is accessible only by sea and water taxi is usually a quicker and more scenic method of travel to places like Te Mahia on Kenepuru Sound (right).

The abundant sunshine, long autumns and cool winters combined with suitable soils make the Wairau Valley one of New Zealand's premier grape growing areas, home to about 70 wineries. The region is particularly famous for its world-class sauvignon blanc.

The Nelson Region

Anchorage

Wainui Bay

Anchorage

In the north-west corner of the South Island, the sunny Nelson area is blessed with mountains, fertile valleys and a glittering coastline.

The Abel Tasman National Park is renowned for its emerald-coloured water, unusual rock formations, golden sandy beaches and varied wildlife. The best ways to see the park are by 52km coastal track or sea kayak.

At Nelson Lakes National Park, the Southern Alps form a dramatic backdrop to the glacier-carved Lake Rotoiti.

Lake Rotoiti

Kaikoura

The Seaward Kaikoura Ranges almost reach the sea at Kaikoura and form a dramatic, often snow-capped backdrop to the town. Just one kilometre from the shore the sea bed plunges 1000 metres down to the Hikurangi Trench, the upwelling of nutrients from this trench providing a rich habitat for a variety of marine mammals such as whales, dolphins and seals. Marine birds like the majestic royal albatross, with a wingspan over 3 metres, feast on the fish attracted by the nutrient-rich waters.

The first whaling station was established in 1843 and by 1850 over 100 men were employed in the industry in Kaikoura alone. However, the emphasis now is totally on conservation and there is a flourishing industry taking tourists to view whales and swim with dolphins or fur seals.

Christchurch

In England in 1848 the Canterbury Association planned to form a Church of England colony that looked just like home. Subsequently the first of 792 Canterbury Pilgrims arrived in four ships in 1850 and began to build a city that today remains faithful to the plan. In 1856 Christchurch was the first city to be declared in New Zealand. Today with a population of 350,000, the most English of New Zealand's cities is the third-largest in the country and the largest on the South Island. It is a blend of old and new architecture, built around the Avon River and surrounded by 150 hectares of parkland. In the centre of the city, Cathedral Square is dominated by Christ Church Cathedral, conceived in 1850, but only completed in 1904.

Canterbury

The Canterbury Plains is a patchwork of agricultural fields punctuated by braided streams flowing down from the snow-capped mountains of the Southern Alps.

To the east of Christchurch, the Banks Peninsula was formed by the violent eruptions of two volcanoes, the two craters filling to form the picturesque Lyttleton and Akaroa Harbours. The township of Akaroa has Maori, French and English heritage and the French influence can still be seen. Around the peninsula, small pods of the playful Hector's Dolphins can easily be seen bow-riding, playing with seaweed or leaping from the sea.

Aoraki / Mt Cook

Fittingly for New Zealand's highest mountain, the Maori name for Mt Cook is "Aoraki", which means "cloud piercer". As the Indo-Australian plate pushes under the Pacific one, tectonic forces continue to raise its height by about 7mm per year. Aoraki / Mt Cook is 3754m high, 10m lower than it was in 1991 when approximately 10 million cubic metres of rock and ice fell off the top.

The turquoise colour of the lakes in the region is due to the microscopic rock particles suspended in the glacial melt. The small stone "Church of the Good Shepherd" overlooks Lake Tekapo and features an altar window which frames an outstanding view of the lake and surrounding mountains.

Queenstown

Thousands flocked to the Queenstown district in 1862 when gold was discovered in the Shotover River. The river was very lucrative and on just one day yielded 57.6 kg of gold. The government bought the town in 1863, pronouncing it "fit for a queen", hence its name. Queenstown is built around an inlet of Lake Wakatipu, with stunning views across the lake to the aptly-named Remarkables mountain range. Today it is a mecca for adventure tourism with activities like snow skiing, jet boating, bungy jumping, mountain biking and tramping attracting 1.3 million visitors a year.

Glenorchy

The beautiful settlement of Glenorchy lies at the top of Lake Wakatipu. The famed Routeburn Track starts near here, linking the Mt. Aspiring and Fiordland national parks. Along the track, trekkers enjoy spectacular alpine scenery, beech forest, ice-blue waterfalls, rivers and lakes.

Dunedin

The New Zealand Company selected Otago Harbour as the site for a Scottish settlement in 1840. When gold was discovered in 1861 Dunedin became the country's biggest city, but now it is the fifth-largest and the second-largest in the South Island. The legacy of the gold rush affluence remains with magnificent Victorian and Edwardian architecture. It is the furtherest city in the world from London (19,100 km).

Dunedin sits on the hills surrounding the head of Otago Harbour, which is the remnant of an extinct volcano. It is the home of the University of Otago, the oldest university in New Zealand, founded in 1869.

The Otago Peninsula abounds with wildlife, containing the world's only mainland Royal Albatross colony and several penguin and seal colonies.

The Catlins

The far south-east corner of New Zealand is known as The Catlins. Here the relentless sea and winds have carved the coastline into dramatic cliffs, windswept headlands, blowholes, sea caves and sandy beaches.

The Catlins coast is a common haunt of Hooker's Sea Lions, one of only five species of sea lions in the world. These can dive up to 600m, deeper than any other of the world's sea lions or fur seals.

The picturesque McLean Falls is reached after a walk through one of the many large areas of native forest consisting of rimu, rata, kamahi and silver beech trees.

Stewart Island / Rakiura

About 30km across Foveaux Strait lies Stewart Island / Rakiura, New Zealand's southern-most and third-largest island, with a population of just 400, most of whom live in the settlement of Oban. The island's economy is mainly dependent on fishing and tourism.

Because of it isolation, many bird species thrive here, safe from predators. All introduced vermin such as deer and rats have been eradicated from nearby Ulva Island and endangered birds like the South Island saddleback and Stewart Island robin have been brought back from the brink of extinction. There are estimated to be 20,000 brown kiwi on Stewart Island.

About 250km of walking tracks traverse the dense forest, headlands, sheltered bays and beaches of the isolated island, 80% of which has been set aside for the Rakiura National Park.

Fiordland

In the south-west corner of New Zealand is the wild, spectacularly beautiful and virtually uninhabited region known as Fiordland. Here the west coast is deeply indented by 14 fiords, which are drowned glacial valleys. The best known, Milford Sound is 15 kilometres long and surrounded by sheer, rainforest-clad rock faces that rise 1200 metres or more on either side. One of these, Mitre Peak rises 1695 metres straight out of the sea. This is the wettest part of the country, with annual rainfall of nearly 7 metres on 182 days of the year creating dozens of temporary waterfalls which cascade down the cliff faces from high above.

The fiords contain two distinct layers of water that do not mix. The top few metres of dark tannin-coloured fresh water allow very little light to reach the layer of cold, denser seawater underneath, allowing many deep-water species to grow in shallow waters. The fiords are home to many seals, penguins and bottlenose dolphins which play host to the 550,000 visitors per year.

Doubtful Sound

Mitre Peak and Milford Sound

Westland

Within a short distance, the Southern Alps drop sharply from over 3000 metres to sea level on the west coast, bringing with them the Franz Josef and Fox Glaciers. Fuelled by 5 metres of precipitation each year, these glaciers almost rush at ten times the speed of similar glaciers, ending in temperate rainforest just a few hundred metres from sea level.

Fed by 4 alpine glaciers, Fox Glacier (pictured) falls 2,600 metres on its 13 kilometre journey from the Southern Alps down to the coast.

These glaciers have retreated over 3 kilometres since Captain Cook saw them in 1750, but have been advancing since 1985 at an amazing rate of up to 70 centimetres per day.

Credits

All photographs by Mike Calder, except these:

Skytower, p6: Christopher Howey, Dreamstime.com
Mt Taranaki, p17: David Lloyd, Dreamstime.com
Gannet, p19: David Lloyd, Dreamstime.com
Rotorua Museum, p23: Harris Shiffman, Dreamstime.com
Maori tribal patterns (x2), p30: Nicolette Neish, Dreamstime.com
Carving of warrior, p31: Wendy Kaveney, Dreamstime.com
Maori waka, p31: Danox, Dreamstime.com
Marae, p31: Christopher Howey, Dreamstime.com
Kiwi chick, p32: PhotoNewZealand
Weka, p32: Holger Mette, Dreamstime.com
Lake Rotoiti, p41: Btmo, Dreamstime.com
Mt Cook, p48: Ashley Whitworth, Dreamstime.com
Lake Tekapo, p48: Frederik Green, Dreamstime.com
Queenstown, p50: Ron Summers, Dreamstime.com
Queenstown couple, p50: Ximagination, Dreamstime.com